IPHIGENIA
IN AULIS
BY EURIPIDES

Adapted by Edward Einhorn

Illustrated by Eric Shanower

image®

Book design by Eric Shanower, Edward Einhorn, and Cornelia Wu.

Age of Bronze graphic novels and comic
books by Eric Shanower are available
wherever books and comics are sold and at:
www.age-of-bronze.com

Age of Bronze
is a trademark
of Eric Shanower

Other plays by Edward Einhorn, including
his translation of *Lysistrata*, can be found
on the websites:
www.theater61press.com
and www.edwardeinhorn.com

TO CORNELIA WU

ON STAGE CHARACTERS
(IN ORDER OF APPEARANCE)

AGAMEMNON
OLD SERVANT
MENELAUS
KLYTEMNESTRA
IPHIGENIA
ACHILLES

WOMEN OF CHALKIS/CHORUS
(THREE OR MORE WOMEN,
INCLUDING CHORUS LEADER)

ORESTES (A BABY)

TABLE OF CONTENTS

THA

Mount
Olympus
△

Kyphus.

Mount
Ossa △

Mount
Pelion △

SK

PHTHIA

ITHAKA

LANDS
of

Delphi

EUBOEA

Aulis

the

ACHAEANS

•Thebes
ATTICA

Sikyon•

•Athens

Elis

Corinth

Mycenae•

Tiryns•

Argos•

•Nauplia

SALAMIS

Pylos•

•Sparta
LAKEDAEMON

Map of the
**BRONZE AGE
AEGEAN**

CRETE

Kno

MEDITERRANEAN
SEA

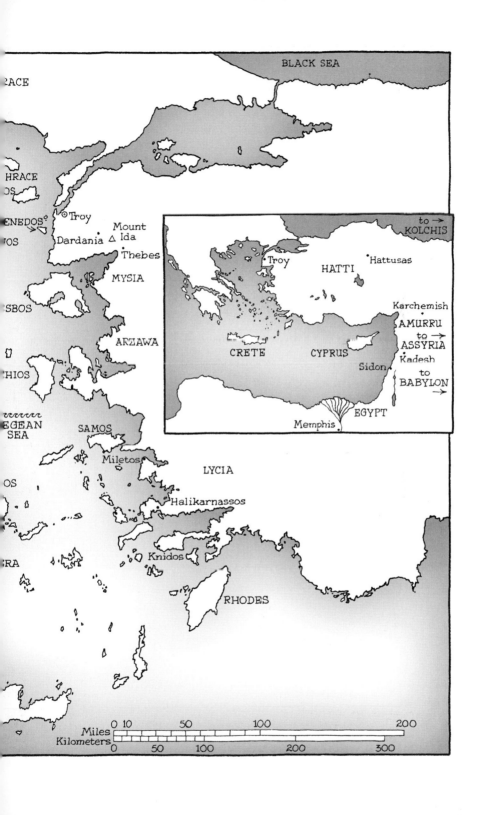

BLACK SEA

RACE

HRACE
OS

ENEDOS
OS

○Troy

Dardania

Mount
△ Ida

• Thebes

MYSIA

ARZAWA

SBOS

HIOS

EGEAN
SEA

SAMOS

Miletos

OS

RA

LYCIA

Halikarnassos

Knidos

RHODES

to →
KOLCHIS

• Troy

HATTI

• Hattusas

Karchemish

AMURRU
to →
ASSYRIA

Kadesh

to
BABYLON
→

Sidon

CRETE

CYPRUS

EGYPT

Memphis

Miles
Kilometers

0 10	50	100	200

0	50	100	200	300

INTRODUCTION/TRANSLATION NOTES

An introduction and some technical notes about the translation/
adaptation. For more thematic thoughts about the play, read the
Director's Note, in Appendix B.

I have always envisioned this project as a play on paper. When I
was young and didn't have the opportunity to go to the theater too
often, I would often just read scripts. Sometimes, to envision them, I
would take toy figures and act them out. But mostly, I would have to
imagine what the play would be, if I saw it.

Then one day, in a used bookstore, I found a copy of Eugène
Ionesco's *The Bald Soprano*, in a "typographical interpretation"
by Robert Massin, using Nicolas Bataille's Paris production as an
inspiration. It was a revelation. The book used black and white
images of the actors from the show, a variety of typefaces, and
some brilliant graphic design to portray not only the words of the
script but also Ionesco's chaotic, playful style. I felt like the book
was a show in itself, in many ways equal to seeing a high quality
performance.

Ever since, I have wanted to try a similar experiment. When Eric
told me he was interested in combining his *Age of Bronze* graphic
images with a new translation of the play, I jumped at it.

Then we both became involved in other things. Meanwhile, my
translation was produced at La MaMa, in New York, which gave me
a chance to develop it. Though it also led to a new version.

In fact, this script has three versions. What you will be reading here is the original version, written to be transformed into a graphic novel/script hybrid, as you see. The other two versions are available online, at iphigeniainaulis.com. Version B was written in anticipation of the stage production, and Version C reflects the stage production as it actually evolved.

What I discovered in the theater is that my directorial interpretation needed some tweaks for the more contemporary style we were using for the chorus members. So almost all the changes are focused on the chorus. Moreover, Aldo Perez, who wrote the music, ended up rewriting the lyrics, which are part of Version C.

Yet the original version continues to seem most appropriate for the book. It matches Eric's style, which is based on intense historical research and combined with his own invention. This version is the closest to what I would call a translation, rather than an adaptation, but that comes with a series of caveats. My version of the script was made with the help of Perseus, an online archive, and also after consulting a number of old translations. And there are still some adaptive decisions I made, in the stage directions, in some choral edits, and especially in the Prologue and the Epilogue (Scene 6).

The Prologue doesn't exist, as such, in most translations. The text is shoehorned into Scene 1, mirroring the existing manuscripts of the drama. But it seems clear that Euripides' original did in fact have a prologue, and dramatically it seems the stronger choice to put the exposition in its traditional space upfront. So I excised it and then bridged the gap in the text with an extra line for the Servant, for clarity.

It may well be that Scene 1 is the work of another author, but since it works dramatically, I did not attempt to remove it.

As for the Epilogue, there is good evidence that the ambivalence of the ending I used was a later addition. Euripides used the *deus ex machina* technique freely, and Artemis may well have literally stepped in to save Iphigenia. This seems much less interesting to me, so I kept the more ambivalent ending. Furthermore, I made the messenger who brings the news the original Servant, to finish his character arc. In the original text, as with all ancient Greek drama, no character is specifically attached to any line of dialogue. Thus, the translator has the freedom to decide who is speaking. But having the Servant say those lines is an unusual choice.

I also have the Servant lead Iphigenia to her sacrifice, another unusual choice made for dramatic reasons.

And interpretive moments abound throughout the book. Eric drew the original illustrations for *Age of Bronze* and suggested the ones he thought would be most appropriate for this book. I helped arrange those illustrations (and a few he didn't suggest), in order to express what I felt was the thrust of the emotion in the moment. In many ways, making those decisions felt similar to directing the play.

I hope, when reading it, the words come to life, thanks to Eric's work. There is no substitute for live theater, but this play on paper is, I think, its own experience, very different than reading an unadorned script.

IPHIGENIA IN AULIS

IPHIGENIA IN AULIS

PROLOGUE

*(AGAMEMNON is in front of his
hut, on the sands of the beach at
Aulis. Nearby, a huge fleet of warships
is anchored. AGAMEMNON is
writing on a tablet, by lamplight.
He finishes and speaks.)*

14

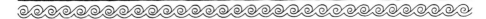

AGAMEMNON

I am Agamemnon. My wife Klytemnestra was one of three daughters born to Leda, daughter of Thestius, the other two being Phoebe and Helen. As Helen was the most beautiful of the three, she had every young man of any distinction in Achaea vying for her hand. The competition frequently became so violent that some of her suitors came close to murdering each other. Helen's father wasn't sure how he could choose a suitor, and he began to wonder whether he should marry her off at all. Finally, a solution

15

came to him. He made all of Helen's suitors take an unbreakable oath. They joined hands, poured offerings of wine, and burned a sacrifice. "Whoever wins Helen as his wife," they swore, "will have our allegiance. Should any man try to steal Helen away from her husband, we will all join as one to chase him down, whoever he is, whether Achaean or foreign, and we will make war upon his city until it is burned

      to

         the

            ground."

Once Helen's father had cleverly engineered this oath, he told his daughter to go wherever love's sweet breath might lead. It led her to my brother, Menelaus, though I dearly wish it hadn't.

After some time, a Trojan man named Paris arrived in Sparta. It was said that Paris had once judged a beauty contest in which Aphrodite herself had taken part. He was dressed in elaborate barbarian robes, covered with jewels and flowers.

He declared his love for Helen. She declared her love for him.

So, while Menelaus was occupied elsewhere,

Paris stole away with Helen, bringing her to Troy.

Menelaus was beside himself in fury. He roared through Achaea and demanded that all of Helen's onetime suitors should remember their oath and help him hunt down Paris. Soon all of Achaea was in arms.

And now here we are at the straits of Aulis, with our ships, our troops, our horses, and our armaments. Because Menelaus is my brother, I have been given the honor of being the general. It is an honor I would gladly give away, if I could.

But we cannot move from here. The wind thwarts us. We cannot sail. In despair, we turned to Kalchas, a great prophet, who told us there is only one hope, if we wished to ever leave this place:

"Your daughter, Iphigenia, must be sacrificed to Artemis. Then, and only then, will the wind blow you in the direction of Troy, which will fall beneath your might."

"Sound the trumpet," I told my herald. "Our war is done. I will not kill my daughter." But my brother overwhelmed me with his pleas and his demands until I agreed to commit this horror, this unspeakable act. I sent a message to my wife. It told her to bring our daughter here to Aulis. I wrote that Iphigenia would be wed to Achilles, our greatest soldier. I wrote that Achilles would not sail with us unless he was married to my own daughter, unless he could one day go home to her. It was a lie, a fake marriage, a base trick. Only Kalchas, Odysseus, Menelaus, and I know the truth. And now I realize that I have made a grave error, an error that must immediately be remedied.

SCENE 1

AGAMEMNON
Old man! Old man, come here! Here, to me.

OLD SERVANT
I am coming, King Agamemnon. What has happened?

AGAMEMNON
Come quickly!

OLD SERVANT
I am coming as quickly as I can.

> (*AGAMEMNON picks up the tablet, looks at it. The OLD SERVANT enters, unnoticed. AGAMEMNON throws the tablet down and holds his head in his hands. AGAMEMNON picks up the tablet, looks at it and looks at the sky, not noticing the OLD SERVANT until he speaks.*)

I was wide awake anyway. At my age, my eyes don't close at night.

AGAMEMNON
What star is that I see?

OLD SERVANT
It is Sirius, the dog star, swiftly pursuing the seven Pleiades.

AGAMEMNON
Everything has become so silent. The birds, the sea, even the wind make no sound.

OLD SERVANT
Then what has disturbed you from your rest, my king? All is calm and quiet. The guards are as still as statues. Why not go back inside?

AGAMEMNON
I envy you, old man. I envy any man who lives an anonymous life. I have never envied those who are famous or powerful.

OLD SERVANT
But those are the men who live lives of glory.

AGAMEMNON
Yes, but that glory is just a trap. It is sweet for a moment, but painful thereafter. Sometimes it is the gods who destroy you, and sometimes it is vicious hordes of mortal men.

OLD SERVANT

It disturbs me to hear such words from a noble king.
Agamemnon, you are the son of Atreus, and he did not bring you
into the world to pursue happiness alone. You are a man, and like
all men, must experience both joy and sorrow. Whether you wish
it or not, it is the will of the gods.

But I notice that you
have something in your
hand, a tablet, and that
your lamp is lit. You've
written a message. You
take your tablet and you
throw it to the ground,
you pick it up, and you
weep. You are like a
man who has lost his
reason. My king, please
tell what drives you to
such despair. I am your
loyal servant. I have
been with you since your
marriage, and I was
picked by your bride's
father for my honesty.
You can trust me.

AGAMEMNON

Yes, you are a loyal servant, loyal to both my wife and me. Go.
Take this message. Take it to my wife in Argos.

OLD SERVANT

Tell me what it says. Then if she asks me to repeat it, I will be able to assure her she reads truly.

(AGAMEMNON reads the tablet.)

AGAMEMNON

"Klytemnestra, ignore what I wrote to you in my last message. Listen to this only. Do not bring your daughter here to Aulis. The wind has died, and there is not even a wave that touches the shore. We will find a more auspicious time for her marriage to Achilles."

OLD SERVANT

What will you do when Achilles learns you have deprived him of his bride? He will be furious with you and Klytemnestra.

This is a dangerous decision.

AGAMEMNON

We have used his name, but Achilles knows nothing of this plan, this marriage, nothing of what I have said about giving him my daughter in marriage.

OLD SERVANT

Then your promise to marry Iphigenia to the son of a goddess—

AGAMEMNON

Was merely an excuse to fetch her here, so she could be sacrificed for the good of Achaea.

OLD SERVANT

A bold and terrible deed.

AGAMEMNON

A horror! By all the gods, a horror, I have gone mad. I am heading to my ruin. Go, quickly, as fast as your old legs can manage.

OLD SERVANT

I shall, my king.

AGAMEMNON

Do not pause to drink or rest or sleep.

OLD SERVANT

How could you think it?

AGAMEMNON

Stop at every fork of the road and look to be sure that no carriage rolls past you, carrying my daughter here to the harbor.

OLD SERVANT

I promise you, I will.

AGAMEMNON

If you see them on the way, make them turn back, send them at full speed towards Mycenae, to stay inside the walls the Cyclops built.

OLD SERVANT

What will make them trust me when I tell them to turn back?

(*AGAMEMNON hands the old servant his ring.*)

AGAMEMNON

My seal. They know it. Keep this letter safe. Now go. Already the sun's fire begins to light the sky. Go. I am depending on your help.

(OLD SERVANT exits offstage.)

No mortal can truly live a life of happiness. We are all fated to face misery, given time.

> *(AGAMEMNON exits into his hut.)*

CHORAL INTERLUDE 1

*(CHORUS of women from Chalkis
enters from offstage.)*

CHORUS

Here I have arrived,
here on the sandy beaches of Aulis,
here I stand after crossing the straits of Euripus,
after leaving my city of Chalkis,
home of the famed springs of Arethusa,
here I stand so that I might behold the Achaean army,
so that I can see the heroes my husband told me of,
see Menelaus, whose hair shines so brightly,
see noble Agamemnon
and see their ships with oars reaching out like wings,
the thousand ships that seek for Helen,
Helen who was taken by the cowherd Paris,
Helen, a gift to Paris from the goddess Aphrodite,

the goddess who once bathed herself in the fountain,
so that Paris could judge her beauty alongside Athena and Hera,
and finally prized her beauty above all.
Here I ran through the grove of Artemis
where I saw the altar, ready for a sacrifice,
here I saw the soldiers' camp,
their dwellings, their steeds, and their armaments,
and felt my cheeks grow red with youthful modesty.
Here I saw Achilles, speeding swiftly on the sands,
testing his speed against the horses,
four great horses, bringing with them a chariot,
Eumelus their driver pressing his steeds forward with his cries,
two gray stallions whose manes were flecked with white,
and two with hair like flames that bore the golden yoke.
Yet all the while Achilles, in full armor, ran victorious in front.
Here I found the wondrous fleet,
which would fill any woman's eyes with pleasure:
fifty lean ships from Phthia,
bearing statues of the sea god's daughters;
sixty from Athens,
the goddess Athena mounted on the prow,
with her chariot drawn by winged horses;
fifty from Boeotia,
Kadmus holding a dragon of gold aloft in their sterns;
one hundred from Mycenae,
home of the Cyclops,
home of Agamemnon and Menelaus,
bringing vengeance to the bride who abandoned them
to make love to a barbarian.

The galleys followed,
the Aenian ships from Lord Guneus,
the white oared Taphian ships,

commanded by King Meges of the dreaded isles of Echinae,
and the nimble ships led by Ajax,
the pride of the Isle of Salamis,
his ships resting so close to me that I could hear the crew.
I have seen the whole fleet,
and no barbarian who sees it can have hope.
I have seen it all and I will remember it all,
when they tell of it I will remember.

SCENE 2

(MENELAUS and OLD SERVANT enter, wrestling with the tablet.)

OLD SERVANT

Menelaus, this is outrageous! You have no right!

MENELAUS

Get away from me! You are too loyal to your master.

OLD SERVANT

It is an honor that you think so.

MENELAUS

You'll regret it if you continue to interfere!

OLD SERVANT

You had no right to look at the message I was carrying.

32

MENELAUS
And you had no right to be carrying a message that will bring harm to all your countrymen.

OLD SERVANT
Argue that question with others, but give me the tablet.

MENELAUS
I will not let go.

OLD SERVANT
Neither shall I.

MENELAUS
I will break your head open with my scepter.

OLD SERVANT
Then I will have had a glorious death, serving my master.

MENELAUS
Let go! You talk too much for a slave!

(MENELAUS wrests the tablet away from the OLD SERVANT.)

OLD SERVANT

Agamemnon! Help! This man has stolen your tablet from me, and he won't listen to reason!

(AGAMEMNON enters.)

AGAMEMNON

What is all this commotion?

MENELAUS

I have the right to speak. He has none.

AGAMEMNON
You, Menelaus? What led you into an argument with this old man? Why are you being so violent with him?

(AGAMEMNON motions for the OLD SERVANT to leave. He does.)

MENELAUS

Look me in the eyes.

Then I will begin to tell you, Agamemnon.

AGAMEMNON

Do you think I am afraid to look at you? I am a son of Atreus.

MENELAUS

Then look at this tablet. Look at this treason!

AGAMEMNON

I am looking. Give it to me.

MENELAUS

No, not until I show it to every Achaean soldier here.

AGAMEMNON

So, you have read my message, and now you know what you have no right to know.

MENELAUS

Yes, to your shame, I have discovered your betrayal.

AGAMEMNON

What lowly trick did you use to discover my servant's task?

MENELAUS

I was waiting for your daughter to arrive from Argos.

AGAMEMNON
How contemptible! What right do you have to spy on my affairs?

MENELAUS
I wanted to do it, so I did. I am not your slave.

AGAMEMNON
This is beyond tolerance! You will not let me govern my own house?

MENELAUS
No, because you are not to be trusted. Not now, not ever.

AGAMEMNON
You are very clever with your quick retorts. There's nothing worse than wickedness dressed with a ready wit.

MENELAUS
You bark at me because you want to evade the truth: that you are unreliable, that your mind changes from one moment to the next. But let me speak, and I promise I will not be too harsh with you. You remember, when we first set out for Troy, how eager you were to lead—yes, I know you made a pretense of indifference, but I knew what was in your heart. How humble you were, unlocking your door so that every common man could enter, taking them each by hand, even those who did not wish it, and offering each of them the opportunity to talk to you. You hoped that this show of openness would win the hearts of the citizens. Then, as soon as you had secured your position, suddenly you were not so available to everyone who called, you dropped the friends who were not use-ful to you, and you hardly stayed at home at all. But a true man

does not change who he is when he finds success, he stays loyal to his friends and helps them when he himself has profited.

This is the first way in which I have found your actions dishonorable. Then, here in Aulis, you became helpless and impotent when the wind grew uncooperative. You were nothing without the help of the gods. Your countrymen demanded to return home, and I saw your face fall in disappointment. How distressed you were that you might lose your opportunity to lead a thousand ships to Troy.

"What should I do?" you asked me. "What plan can we devise?" You were willing to do anything, just so you would not miss your chance at glory. So when Kalchas suggested that the fleet would sail if you sacrificed your daughter, you were happy, yes, overjoyed to agree.

AGAMEMNON
I was forced to it!

MENELAUS
So you claim now, but you sent your messenger by your own volition. It was you, too, who thought up the tale of the marriage to Achilles. And now you have sent a new message, to gainsay the first? Now you have decided you will not be your daughter's murderer? Well, the gods have witnessed your duplicity. Countless men, like you, have risen high only to meet failure, some at the hands of foolish men, some deserving their fate for failing at their duty to keep their cities safe. Good connections do not make a good leader. You must show a good mind and good sense.

AGAMEMNON

Now I will speak. And when I speak, I will not raise my head too
high, and I will speak with modesty, as a brother should speak to
a brother. Tell me, why do you stare at me with bloodshot eyes
while you huff and puff with fury? Who has wronged you? What
do you want? A virtuous wife? I cannot give you one. You had
enough trouble controlling the one you had. Must I pay for your
mistakes? You are not bothered by my supposed ambition. You
are bothered by the fact that you can't hold a beautiful woman in
your arms. For her, you've abandoned common decency. You've
degraded yourself for base pleasures. And is it mad of me to turn
and realize I have committed a terrible mistake? No, you're the
one who is mad. You're mad for wanting back this wife of yours.
The gods have been kind enough to take her off your hands. Yes,
her suitors were so eager for her that they swore her father's oath.
The goddess of foolish hopes led them to that pledge. And now
they feel compelled to honor it. But an oath elicited through force
or trickery is not an oath at all. No, I will not slay my children. I
will not spend my days and nights in tears so that you can punish
your worthless wife. That is all I have to say to you. I think it is
easy to understand. If you choose not to listen, that is your choice.
But I must do as my conscience tells me.

40

CHORUS LEADER
You have changed your mind, but for the better. It is a noble desire to keep one's child from harm.

MENELAUS
I see I am alone and friendless.

AGAMEMNON
You have friends. But do not try to destroy them.

MENELAUS
Will you not prove to me you are my brother?

AGAMEMNON

Behave like a friend and brother to me, do me good instead of harm.

MENELAUS

For your daughter, you are determined to abandon every other Achaean?

AGAMEMNON

Both you and Achaea are the victims of some god's hatred.

MENELAUS

What a proud king you must be, now that you've abandoned your brother. I will find help elsewhere, from other friends.

(MESSENGER enters.)

MESSENGER

King Agamemnon, commander of all Achaea! I have brought you your daughter, Iphigenia, your wife, Klytemnestra, and your baby boy, Orestes! May the sight of them give you great joy, after their long absence! They are resting and bathing their feet, after the long journey. Their mares are in the pasture, grazing. Their arrival has created great excitement among the soldiers. Everyone wants to see those whom fortune has so blessed. "Is there going to be a wedding?" they ask. "Or does King Agamemnon love his child so deeply that he cannot bear to be away from her?" Others have noticed that offerings are being made to Artemis, but wonder, if she is to be a bride, who is to be her bridegroom? Come, let us celebrate! King Menelaus, prepare for the marriage feast! Put a garland on your head, King Agamemnon! Let us play the pipes and dance!

Today is a happy day for your girl!

AGAMEMNON

Thank you for your news. Now go inside. All will be well. All that is fated to be well will be well.

(*MESSENGER exits.*)

How can I speak, for misery? How can I even begin? I have been caught in the net of fate. I planned, but the gods planned more craftily. How lucky are those who are low born. They can at least weep without hesitation. But a king must show dignity, even in the darkest times. We are slaves to the people we rule. I cannot weep, but I cannot fail to weep, for failing to weep at such a time is sickness.

(AGAMEMNON has given in to tears.)

What will I say to my wife when I see her? How can I look at her, welcome her, let her see into my eyes? I did not intend to invite her here, too. Why did she have to come? It will be my undoing.

But of course she is here, what mother would not accompany a daughter so treasured to her wedding? So this is how my wife will learn of my betrayal.

And my poor maiden daughter—why do I call her that?—she will not be long a maiden, now that Hades will take her for his bride. I can hear her pleading to me piteously: "Father? Can you truly mean to kill me? Then I hope you and everyone you love is married to Death, as I am today." And my baby Orestes will be there, too young to even walk, but not too young to scream and cry, not too young for me to know the meaning of his cries. Oh, what destruction Paris has brought! It is he and Helen who set this all in motion!

CHORUS LEADER
Even I, a foreigner, lament for this king.

MENELAUS
Brother, give me your hand.

*(AGAMEMNON gives
him his hand.)*

AGAMEMNON
You may have it. You have won, and I must bear my misery.

MENELAUS
I swear by Atreus our
father, and Pelops his
father, that now I will
say just what is in my
heart, without any
subterfuge or evasion.
When I saw you weep,
I wept. I take back my
former words. I am
with you. You must
not kill your child.
Not for my sake. I
cannot see you grieve
her death while my

children still give me pleasure. What good would it do me? Would
it bring me a wife? I can marry again. Shall I destroy my brother to
bring back Helen, destroy a man I treasure to bring back a wicked
woman? I was being rash and childish. But now I understand what a
thing it is to kill one's own child. And she is my own niece, she who
would lose her life to bring back Helen. What is Helen to her? Let's
abandon this mission, disband our army, and go home. Brother, do
not cry. It makes me cry as well. It is your concern what the oracles
say, not mine. I give you any interest I may have had in it.

You see, my threats and anger are gone. I have changed. It's only natural to change, when you love your brother. It is the right thing to do.

CHORUS LEADER

Your words are noble and worthy of your ancestor Tantalus, the son of Zeus himself.

AGAMEMNON

Thank you, Menelaus. I had lost hope that you would say those words to me.

MENELAUS

I hate it when brotherly love is infected with bitterness. Too often inheritance or a dispute over love stands between brothers.

AGAMEMNON

But I have no choice now. I must kill my girl.

MENELAUS
What? Who will force you to kill your child?

AGAMEMNON
The entire assembled army.

MENELAUS
Not if you send her back to Argos.

AGAMEMNON
Perhaps I could manage to send her back in secret. But there is one thing that cannot be kept secret from the soldiers.

MENELAUS
You cannot live in fear of the mob.

AGAMEMNON
Kalchas will tell them what the oracle prophesied.

MENELAUS
He won't speak if he's dead,
and we can see to that.

AGAMEMNON
Yes, there's a whole tribe of these prophets, and they are an
ambitious lot.

MENELAUS
Half of what they say is useless, and the rest just brings misery.

AGAMEMNON
But there's something else that worries me. Does it worry you, too?

MENELAUS
What? You have to tell me what it is.

AGAMEMNON
The son of Sisyphus knows everything.

MENELAUS
Odysseus? He will do us no harm.

AGAMEMNON
He is unreliable. He loves being popular with the masses.

MENELAUS
It is power he loves. It is an evil addiction.

AGAMEMNON
I can see him telling the soldiers the whole story, every word that Kalchas said, and how I offered Artemis a victim then reneged. He will tell the army to kill us both and then slaughter the girl, and if we run to Argos, they will raze it to the ground, Cyclopean walls and all. This is the trap in which I am ensnared. Almighty gods, how helpless you have made me! But if this must be, do me one favor, Menelaus. Make sure Klytemnestra knows nothing, at least until the deed is done and my girl has gone to Hades. I need no more tears than necessary.

And you, women of Chalkis, make sure you speak nothing of this either.

(AGAMEMNON and MENELAUS exit.)

CHORAL INTERLUDE 2

CHORUS
Blessed are they who lie upon Aphrodite's couch,
feeling love with moderation,
desire with self-control.
Eros shoots two arrows,
one delivers happiness when it strikes,
the other delivers bewilderment.
Oh Kypris, most lovely goddess,
keep confusion from my bridal bed.
May I feel passion, but not be ruled by it,
may Aphrodite visit but not stay too long.

Various are the ways of human nature,
but the tenets of human virtue are obvious to all,
especially those who have been well schooled.
There is great wisdom in great modesty,
for it brings grace, good judgment,
and a reputation that is everlasting.
There is nothing nobler than seeking virtue:
for women it is love's secret,
for men it is an asset that brings greatness to their city.

Paris, you were once a cowherd.
You stood among white heifers,
playing barbarous melodies upon your reed pipe,
trying to imitate the nearby Trojans.

There among your fat cattle, three goddesses found you,
and soon fate guided you inside Helen's ivory palace.
Your gazes locked and filled with love,
and that ache of love you felt within your breasts,
that ache has armed these ships,
filling them with spears and soldiers who ache to war with Troy.

53

SCENE 3

*(KLYTEMNESTRA and
IPHIGENIA enter in a chariot.)*

CHORUS

But hail, oh hail!
It is the Princess Iphigenia and her
mother, Klytemnestra, daughter of
Tyndareus! What a noble ancestry they
have! How high they have risen in
fortune! The wealthy seem like gods to
common women like ourselves.

CHORUS LEADER

Women of Chalkis, let us guide this
great queen down from her chariot.
Let us lead her with gentle hands,
so she and her daughter may
descend without fear. Daughter of
Agamemnon, we are strangers here,
like you. Do not be frightened.

KLYTEMNESTRA

Here is good fortune, to be greeted
with such kindness. An auspicious
beginning for a young woman about to
be married. Please be careful with the
gifts I have brought for my daughter's
dowry. My child, step cautiously, the
maidens here will help you down.

54

Someone see to the horses, they grow fearful without soothing. Might one of you give me your hand, so I can descend with some grace? Oh, but hold the baby first. He is Orestes, Agememnon's son. Look, he is asleep, lulled by the movement of the chariot.

Wake up, my dozing prince, it is your sister's wedding day. You will have a new brother today, the son of a sea nymph. Stand next to me, Iphigenia, so these strangers can see how happy we are together.

(*AGAMEMNON enters.*)

Look, it is your father!

(*IPHIGENIA runs to AGAMEMNON and hugs him.*)

IPHIGENIA

Do not be angry with me, Mother, I must hold him first. Oh, Father, I have so yearned to see you again that I must outrun everyone in order to embrace you.

KLYTEMNESTRA

Of course you may. Of all our children, you love your father the most.

IPHIGENIA

I am so glad to see you, Father! How long it has been.

AGAMEMNON

Yes. Your words speak for me too.

IPHIGENIA

Thank you, Father, you were so clever to bring me here to you.

AGAMEMNON

As for that—I cannot say one way or the other.

IPHIGENIA

You say you are happy, but you look so upset.

AGAMEMNON

I have many things on my mind, as kings and generals do.

IPHIGENIA
Think about your daughter, not your worries.

AGAMEMNON
I am thinking only of you, now.

IPHIGENIA
Then smile. Stop knitting up your brow and smile.

AGAMEMNON
You cannot imagine how I feel to see you.

IPHIGENIA
And yet your eyes are filled with tears.

AGAMEMNON
I am thinking of our next parting—it will be a long one.

IPHIGENIA
You should stay at home, Father, with your children.

AGAMEMNON
If only I could. That is what's making me so sad.

IPHIGENIA

Then forget about the war! Forget about Menelaus's troubles. Let the whole thing come to an end.

AGAMEMNON

It is putting an end to me, and to others as well.

IPHIGENIA

You have been here in Aulis such a long time.

AGAMEMNON

And yet I still cannot leave.

IPHIGENIA

Will your voyage be very far?

AGAMEMNON

Your voyage, I think, will be farther. But we will meet again.

IPHIGENIA

I wish you could take me with you.

AGAMEMNON

When you are gone, you will forget all about me.

IPHIGENIA

Will my mother come too, or just me alone?

AGAMEMNON

Alone, without your mother or your father.

IPHIGENIA

Do you mean, in my new home with my husband?

AGAMEMNON

Hush. It is not proper for maidens to speak of such matters.

IPHIGENIA

When you have returned home from Troy, you will have to come straight to me.

AGAMEMNON

Before I leave, I have a sacrifice I must perform.

IPHIGENIA

Of course. The gods need their sacrifices.

AGAMEMNON

You will attend. You will stand right next to the purifying water.

IPHIGENIA
Will we dance round
the altar?

AGAMEMNON
How happy you are in your innocence. But give me a kiss and
your hand, then go inside. I know young girls are shy about having
the world observe them. Soon, you will embark on a trip that
will take you far away from me.

*(IPHIGENIA
kisses him.)*

Oh, to touch your cheek, your hair,
to hold you close . . . how unfair it
is that you have to suffer for Helen
and for Troy. But enough, I must
stop my tears. Go inside.

*(IPHIGENIA
exits.)*

Daughter of Leda, forgive me for my weakness. I know I have shed too many tears over this marriage to Achilles. It is a time of joy, of course, but a father's heart breaks when he sends his daughter to live in a stranger's home.

KLYTEMNESTRA
I feel the same way. I don't blame you for feeling grief. I too will shed some tears when I lead my daughter to her marriage and hear the marriage hymns. But this is a common grief, and it disappears in time. So tell me about the man who is going to wed our daughter. I want to know more about his family.

AGAMEMNON
They say Zeus himself was his great-grandsire. Asopos, the river god, is in his lineage, and his mother Thetis is a nymph, the daughter of Nereus, god of the sea.

KLYTEMNESTRA
Did Peleus marry Thetis with the gods' blessing or against their wishes?

AGAMEMNON
It was Zeus who gave the bride away.

KLYTEMNESTRA
Where was the wedding? In the sea?

AGAMEMNON
At the foot of Mount Pelion, where Cheiron lives.

KLYTEMNESTRA
Where the Centaurs live, they say.

AGAMEMNON
And the gods made them a feast.

KLYTEMNESTRA
Was Achilles raised by Thetis or his father?

AGAMEMNON
By Cheiron, far from wicked men.

KLYTEMNESTRA
A wise tutor, and an even wiser father, to entrust his son.

AGAMEMNON
This is the man who will marry our daughter.

KLYTEMNESTRA
There seems little to find fault with. And where in Achaea does he call home?

AGAMEMNON
He comes from Phthia, overlooking the river Apidanus.

KLYTEMNESTRA
Is this where he will take our daughter?

AGAMEMNON
If he wishes. That will be his
decision, as her husband.

KLYTEMNESTRA
May they find joy in their
marriage. When will it be?

AGAMEMNON
The next full moon will be
the most auspicious time.

KLYTEMNESTRA
What about the sacrifice? Will
it be made?

AGAMEMNON
It will. It is my next task.

KLYTEMNESTRA
With the feast afterwards?

AGAMEMNON
After the required sacrifice. Yes.

KLYTEMNESTRA
And the women's feast? Where
will it be?

AGAMEMNON
Here, by the ships.

KLYTEMNESTRA
I suppose we have no choice.
Yet perhaps it will bring luck.

AGAMEMNON
Remember this: you must obey
me, now.

KLYTEMNESTRA
I always do.

AGAMEMNON
I will take charge of everything. When the bridegroom's here—

KLYTEMNESTRA
Of everything? Will you play the mother's part?

AGAMEMNON
My soldiers and I will take care of this marriage.

KLYTEMNESTRA

And where will I be?

AGAMEMNON

In Argos, caring for our daughters.

KLYTEMNESTRA

What of my eldest daughter? Who
will raise the bridal torch, if
not me?

AGAMEMNON

I will provide all the light needed.

KLYTEMNESTRA

No, these customs are important.
That should not be.

AGAMEMNON

There are only soldiers here. It is not right for you to be alone
among them all.

KLYTEMNESTRA

It is not right for me to be absent during my child's wedding.

AGAMEMNON

Your other daughters need you, at home.

KLYTEMNESTRA
No, by the goddess queen of Argos. Go and take care of what business you need to outside of the home, but it is mine to rule everything inside it. I will go now and help the bride prepare.

(KLYTEMNESTRA exits into the hut.)

AGAMEMNON
Alas, it is no use. I am thwarted in every way. I cannot even get my wife to leave. I try to use trickery to protect those I love most, but my schemes all fail. Now I must face Kalchas and discuss with him the sacrifice he says the goddess demands. It is my duty to my country. A wise man should have a wife he can use for good purpose, or no wife at all.

(AGAMEMNON exits.)

CHORAL INTERLUDE 3

CHORUS

Soon these ships will sail, carrying an army,
travelling through the silver waters of Simois
until they arrive at the rocky shore below Troy.
In that city, I have heard, lives Kassandra,
the princess who shakes with Apollo's prophecies,
her hair swirling round her in the sunlight as she speaks.

The Trojans will stand upon their walls and watch
as the broad prows of the Achaean ships
ride the waves, nearing the Simois rivulets.

They will watch the ships that seek for Helen,
sister to Kastor and Pollux,
the twin children of Zeus
the twin stars in the heavens. May we never feel the fear that the
women will feel in golden Lydia and in Phrygia, near Troy.

May we never stand by our looms and ask,
"Who shall grab hold of my hair
and drag me, weeping, from my home?"
This misery is the fault of the swan's daughter,
the swan that was Zeus in disguise,
if that story of her birth can be believed,
if that story is not merely the invention of frivolous poets.

SCENE 4

(ACHILLES enters.)

ACHILLES

Where is the Achaean commander? Are there any servants here to announce that I, Achilles son of Peleus, am standing here? Not everyone who waits on this beach with you is in the same situation. Some of us have no wives or children, and we have left our homes unattended, because of the passion that the gods have placed in our hearts. It is a passion which has sent our whole nation with you on this journey. I can only speak for myself. Let others speak for themselves. I have travelled from Pharsalus, left behind my father Peleus, and here am I now beside the Euripus, waiting for the whisper of a breeze that blows aright. My Myrmidon soldiers press me, asking "Why do we wait? How much more time must we spend on this expedition to Troy? If we are to do something, lead us to it, or else lead us away from here and away from these two dallying sons of Atreus."

(KLYTEMNESTRA enters.)

KLYTEMNESTRA

Son of the sea nymph, I heard you speak so I came out to see you.

(ACHILLES averts his eyes.)

ACHILLES

Most holy modesty, who is this woman so blessed by beauty?

70

KLYTEMNESTRA
You have not seen me before, so of course you do not know me. I appreciate your reverent modesty.

ACHILLES

But who are you? Why are you, a woman, in this place of men and shields?

KLYTEMNESTRA

I am Klytemnestra, daughter of Leda, wife to Agamemnon.

ACHILLES

Well answered, quick and clear. But it is not seemly for me to talk to women.

(*ACHILLES begins
to leave.*)

KLYTEMNESTRA
Don't leave so quickly.
Stay and join your right
hand with mine, as a
prelude to a happy
marriage.

ACHILLES
Take your hand? What
are you suggesting? I
have no right. I could
never look Agamemnon
in the eyes, if I did.

KLYTEMNESTRA
You have every right, son of the sea nymph. You are marrying
my daughter.

ACHILLES
Marrying your daughter? I . . . don't know what to say. Is this
some delusion?

KLYTEMNESTRA
Men shy away from their new family, when marriage is in the air.
It is natural.

ACHILLES
I have never sought your daughter in marriage, nor have the sons
of Atreus spoken to me about these plans.

KLYTEMNESTRA
How can this be? I am as surprised as you must have been a moment ago.

ACHILLES
Then let's try to find the truth behind it. Perhaps we are both right. It may just be a misunderstanding.

KLYTEMNESTRA
Can I have been deceived? Can this marriage exist only in my mind? I feel so ashamed.

ACHILLES
Maybe someone is playing a trick on us. Pay no attention to it, it doesn't matter.

KLYTEMNESTRA
I must leave. I am humiliated, to have been made into a liar like this.

ACHILLES
I feel the same. But I must go inside to see your husband.

*(OLD SERVANT peeks his
head out from the hut.)*

OLD SERVANT
Wait! Stranger, son of the gods, wait! And you too, daughter
of Leda.

ACHILLES
Who calls us from that half
opened door? He sounds so
frightened.

OLD SERVANT
I am a slave, nothing more.
Why pretend better?

ACHILLES
Whose slave?

OLD SERVANT
That woman's, over there. I was a gift from her father.

ACHILLES
Well, I am still here. What do you want? Why did you stop me?

OLD SERVANT
Are the two of you alone?

ACHILLES
We are alone. Come out from there and speak.

(OLD SERVANT emerges.)

OLD SERVANT
May fortune and my own foresight be enough for those I hope
to save.

ACHILLES
Portentous words, though your point is slow in coming.

*(KLYTEMNESTRA
holds out her hand.)*

KLYTEMNESTRA
Here, take my right
hand. Speak to me.

*(The SERVANT
takes her hand and
kneels before her.)*

OLD SERVANT
You know I am a good man and devoted to you and your children.

KLYTEMNESTRA
I know that you have served my house for many years.

OLD SERVANT
And that King Agamemnon received me as part of your dowry?

KLYTEMNESTRA
Yes, you came with me to Argos, and you have always been my servant.

OLD SERVANT
Yes. So you know I am loyal to you first—you, above your husband.

KLYTEMNESTRA
Come, tell me what you have to say.

OLD SERVANT
It is about your daughter. Her father is about to kill her—

KLYTEMNESTRA

What? What sort of mad story are you telling me?

OLD SERVANT

He will cut her white throat open with his sword.

KLYTEMNESTRA

Are you telling me my husband's gone insane?

OLD SERVANT

No, he is sane, except when it comes to you and your daughter.
There, he is mad.

KLYTEMNESTRA

What reason would he have? What avenging god possesses him?

OLD SERVANT

It is the Oracle, according to Kalchas. So that the fleet may sail.

KLYTEMNESTRA

Where will it sail? Alas for me, alas for the girl whose father waits
to slay her.

OLD SERVANT

To Troy, so Menelaus can bring back Helen.

KLYTEMNESTRA

So Helen's rescue dooms Iphigenia?

OLD SERVANT

Now you know everything. Agamemnon intends to sacrifice her to Artemis.

KLYTEMNESTRA

Then why talk of her marriage to Achilles?

OLD SERVANT

To lure you into bringing your daughter here.

KLYTEMNESTRA

Oh my daughter, this journey we have taken, it will bring death to us both.

OLD SERVANT

I pity the two of you. It is an awful deed that Agamemnon plans.

KLYTEMNESTRA

I am finished. I can't hold back my tears.

OLD SERVANT

Go ahead and weep. What mother would not weep at the loss of her children?

KLYTEMNESTRA

Where did you hear all this? How did you discover it?

OLD SERVANT

I was given a letter which referred to the earlier message
you received.

KLYTEMNESTRA

Did it tell me not to bring my child to her death, or did it urge
me on?

OLD SERVANT

It was meant to prevent you from coming. Your husband
momentarily regained his reason.

KLYTEMNESTRA

And if this is really true, why did you not deliver this letter to me?

OLD SERVANT

Menelaus took it from me. He is to blame for everything.

KLYTEMNESTRA

Son of Peleus and the sea nymph, do you hear all this?

ACHILLES

I hear your misery. I am sorry that my name was used in the matter.

KLYTEMNESTRA

They will murder my daughter. They tricked me by pretending
she would be wed to you.

ACHILLES
I am angry with your husband as well. I do not take this lightly.

(KLYTEMNESTRA kneels in front of ACHILLES and embraces his legs.)

KLYTEMNESTRA
I am not ashamed to fall at your knees. What should be more important to me than the well-being of my daughter? Oh please help me, son of a goddess, help me and help the young bride who was said to be your own, although I know it was a lie. It is for your sake that I placed a bridal wreath upon her head, and when she is murdered, it is you who will be blamed for it. For even though you were never married to her, your name is now connected to this poor maiden's name. I beg you by your hand, by your noble chin, by your own mother. I have been brought so low because of the power of your name, and that is something you are bound to defend. My only altar is your knee. I have no friends here to turn to. You know how heartless Agamemnon has been. I am a woman alone among unruly soldiers, all ready to do the worst to me, useful as they may be otherwise. But if you stretch out your hand and hold us under your protection, we will be safe. If not, we are lost.

CHORUS LEADER
Mothers have a great and mysterious power, every one of them. They will risk anything for their children's sake.

ACHILLES

It seems I have been made into the worst of men, a nothing,
no better than Menelaus in all this, not the son of a king but
of a vengeful demon, for your husband is using my name to

commit murder. By Nereus, father of my
mother Thetis, raised in the waves of the sea,
Agamemnon will not touch your daughter!
No, if he lays even a finger upon her, let the
barbarous Mount Sipylos, home to his ancestors,
be ever considered great, and let the name
of my own Phthia never again be spoken. My
sword will bear witness: it will be covered in
barbarian blood well before we reach Troy if
your daughter is taken from me.

OLD SERVANT

May you be blessed for the rest of your life for helping those
in need!

ACHILLES

Listen to me, and perhaps all will be well.

KLYTEMNESTRA

Go on, I am eager to hear.

ACHILLES

We will try to restore her father back to sanity.

KLYTEMNESTRA

He is too cowardly. He fears the army.

ACHILLES

One argument can win out against another.

KLYTEMNESTRA

That seems a cold hope. But tell me what you propose.

ACHILLES

First you must beg him not to kill his daughter. If he refuses to listen, come to me. But if luck is with you, perhaps things can turnout well for your family even without my aid.

KLYTEMNESTRA

Sensible enough. I will do so. But if my pleas fail to work, how will I find you? Shall I wander forlornly, searching for your hand to clasp in aid?

ACHILLES

I will keep an eye out for you. I will make sure you do not have to run frantically among the soldiers. You will not shame your father's house. Tyndareus is a great man and deserves a good reputation.

KLYTEMNESTRA

I will do as you say. Lead me, and I will follow. If there are gods, they will reward you. If there are not, then perhaps nothing matters.

(KLYTEMNESTRA and the OLD SERVANT go inside the hut and ACHILLES exits.)

CHORAL INTERLUDE 4

CHORUS

What were the marriage hymns they sang,
as the Libyan flutes played
and the lyre led the dance,
and the reeds piped their high melodies?

What were they singing as the Muses
danced,
their feet adorned with golden sandals?
What was sung as they feasted,
to celebrate the marriage of Peleus to
Thetis, the sea nymph?

There on the slopes where the Centaurs
stood,
Ganymedes, whom Zeus delights in,
poured wine into golden cups.
There the fifty daughters of Nereus
whirled round
in a twisting circle for their sister's nuptials.

There the Centaurs, great horsemen crowned with wreaths,
galloped rowdily to the feast,
drinking deeply from Bacchus's bowl,
crying:

"Daughter of Nereus,
Cheiron, Apollo's prophet, foretells
that you will bear a mighty son, the pride of Thessaly.
He will sail to the land where Priam dwells,
bringing Myrmidon soldiers,
to burn down glorious Troy.
There he will wear your gift,
golden armor crafted by the god Hephaistos."

So did the gods bless
the marriage of Peleus
to the eldest of the sea nymphs.

But you, Princess Iphigenia,
your country will crown you
as a cow is crowned before a
knife cuts across its throat.
You were not raised in a field,
near the shepherds' tunes and
the herdsmen's cries.
Your mother raised you to
marry a son of one of the gods.

Where is virtue?
Where is modesty?
The gods have been discarded
and man has left virtue behind.
Lawlessness is our only law.
We no longer work together
to avoid the wrath of the gods.

85

SCENE 5

*(KLYTEMNESTRA
enters from the hut.)*

KLYTEMNESTRA

I am looking for my husband. He has been gone for a long while.
Inside, my daughter wails with sorrow at the news of her
father's plans.

(She spots AGAMEMNON)

It seems I have been speaking of a man who stands nearby. There is
Agamemnon, soon to be condemned for his crimes against his child.

(AGAMEMNON enters.)

AGAMEMNON

Daughter of Leda, I am glad to find you here. I have something to
say to you that I would prefer that the bride did not hear.

*(KLYTEMNESTRA
glares at him.)*

*(AGAMEMNON
hesitates, seeing
her.)*

KLYTEMNESTRA

What do you want to say?

AGAMEMNON

No, call the child to me. The purifying water has been prepared, and the barley stands ready to be cast into the fire. The heifers, who must give their dark blood to Artemis before the wedding, are waiting to be slain.

KLYTEMNESTRA

What pretty words. But I have a harder time finding the words to praise your actions.

(She calls into the hut.)

Come here, my daughter. You know what your father intends.

(IPHIGENIA enters. She is crying.)

Here she is, obedient to you as always. Now, I will speak for us both.

AGAMEMNON

Why are you crying, my girl? Where is the joy I usually see when you look at me? Why do you stare at the ground and hide your face?

KLYTEMNESTRA
Answer my questions truthfully, my husband.

AGAMEMNON
There is no need to command me. You can ask your question.

KLYTEMNESTRA
Are you going to murder our daughter?

AGAMEMNON
What an awful suggestion! How dare you suspect me of such a vile thing?

KLYTEMNESTRA
Calm yourself. Just answer my question.

AGAMEMNON
Ask me a reasonable question and I will give you a reasonable answer.

KLYTEMNESTRA

This is my only question. I want to hear nothing from you except the answer.

AGAMEMNON

Oh gods, why is this my fate?

KLYTEMNESTRA

It is mine too, and hers, the same fate for us all.

AGAMEMNON

How have I wronged you?

KLYTEMNESTRA

How can you ask me that? If this is cleverness, then it is not so clever.

AGAMEMNON

I am lost. I have been betrayed.

KLYTEMNESTRA

I know everything. I know what you intend to do to me.

> *(AGAMEMNON sighs but does not answer.)*

You confess it in your silence and your sighs. You don't need to say anything.

AGAMEMNON

Then I won't say anything. Why add a shameless lie to our misfortunes?

KLYTEMNESTRA

Then listen to me. I will speak plainly, not in riddles. To begin with, you forced yourself on me, marrying me against my will after killing my husband. Your violence pushed my unborn babe out from my womb, and you threw his still body on the ground. When Kastor and Pollux, my twin brothers, came riding in to save me you went begging to my father, who allowed you to take me as your wife.

Yet I made peace with all that, and as your wife I have been blameless, as you yourself can attest. I have been faithful. When you enter your home I give you pleasure, when you are gone I add to your prosperity. Good wives like this are a rarity, while bad wives are in abundance. I bore you a son and three daughters. Now you will break my heart by taking one away from me. If someone asks you why you are planning to kill her, what will you say? Shall I give your answer for you? "So that Menelaus can have Helen back." You will buy a wicked woman back with your own child's life. You will trade someone you love for someone everyone hates.

Consider this: when you sail away to war, leaving me behind, what will be in my heart for all those years? I will see her empty chair, her empty bedroom, sit alone and weep. I will cry out "My child,

your father murdered you with his own hands! It was he and no one else." Will you want to return to a home where you have left us nothing but hatred? What reception will you expect from your daughters and from me? It will be the one you deserve. Do not force me to do something unspeakable, by doing something unspeakable to me.

Imagine yourself sacrificing your daughter. What prayers will you say? What is the blessing you will ask for while slicing your child's throat? A homecoming whose horrors match your shameful departure? And what blessing do you think I will give you? I would have to think the gods fools if I prayed for a man who had slaughtered his own flesh.

Will you kiss your children, when you come back to Argos? No, you will have no right. Will any of your children be able to look at you, knowing you have put one of them to death? Have you even thought about this, or are you too busy thinking about being king and general? Why don't you say this to your soldiers: "My countrymen, do you want to sail to Troy? Then let us all draw lots, and he who loses, his daughter will die." At least that would be more just than simply offering up your own daughter on the altar. Or let Menelaus murder his daughter Hermione for her mother's sake. This is his quarrel. But no, I must lose my child, even though I have been true to you, while my adulterous sister will find her daughter home safe in Sparta. Am I wrong in any way? If not, have the wisdom to spare our daughter.

CHORUS LEADER
Listen to her, Agamemnon, you can join together and save your child, there's no action more honorable. No one would say otherwise.

IPHIGENIA

If I could speak as well as Orpheus, Father, if I could use word to inspire the rocks around us to rise up and follow me, if I had that same gift of persuasion I would use it. But I have only one talent, my tears. I offer them to you. It is all I can do.

(IPHIGENIA kneels in front of him. AGAMEMNON looks away.)

I bend before you like a branch bending towards the earth, pressing my body against your knees. This is the body that your wife gave birth to. Don't send me to an early death. It is sweet to see the sun's light. Do not force me down into the darkness of the Underworld.

I was the first child to call you father, the first you called your child. I was the first to sit upon your knee while you fondly kissed me. You used to say to me, "Will I see you one day, happy in your husband's house, bringing honor to your family?" And I would say to you, as I pulled upon your beard, the same beard I now caress, "And what about you, Father? Will I welcome you into my house, when you are an old man, and take care of you in thanks for all the years that you took care of me?" I remember every word we said, but you have forgotten them, and now you are planning to end my life.

By Pelops, by your father Atreus, by my mother, who suffered the pain of my birth and suffers more pain now, I beg you to spare me.

What do I have to do with the marriage of Paris and Helen?
Why should I die because of them? Look at me, look me in the
eyes and give me a kiss, give me that at least to remember when I
die, if you are determined to remain deaf to my pleas.

CHORUS LEADER
Vile Helen, your marriage has brought such terrible strife to the
House of Atreus.

AGAMEMNON
I love my children. I know when I should be moved to pity. I am
not mad. I am forcing myself to do this terrible deed, because to
not do it would be even more terrible. I have no choice. Look at
this huge fleet of war ships, filled with soldiers covered in bronze.
Yet they cannot sail towards glory on Troy's plains, nor assault its

famed towers, unless I offer you
as a sacrifice. This is what Kalchas,
the prophet, has demanded. Our
soldiers are driven mad by their
desire to sail to the land of those
barbarians, to protect the wives
throughout our country from
abduction. If I refuse to obey the
goddess, they will kill me, and both
of you, and my daughters home in
Argos. It is not Menelaus who has
enslaved me. I am not compelled by him. It is our county, Achaea,
who rules me. It is for her sake that I must sacrifice you. If you and
I can win our county's freedom, then we must. We must not let the
barbarians carry off our wives.

93

(AGAMEMNON kisses
IPHIGENIA and exits.)

KLYTEMNESTRA

Oh you foreign women, oh my child, how my heart breaks at your death. Your father flees from you, having consigned you to Hades.

IPHIGENIA

Oh mother, mother! The very man who fathered me has now abandoned me. I curse the day I first saw you, Helen, for you have  doomed me to die an unholy death at the hands of my unholy father. I wish that Aulis had never allowed in these bronze-beaked ships, intent on Troy, or that Zeus had not blown the wind that halts them here. For some, Zeus brings joy with his breath, filling their sails, for others he brings sadness, flaccid sails, and delay. What suffering, what terrible suffering we creatures who spend our brief moments on this earth must endure. It is our fate.

CHORUS LEADER

Curse you, Helen, for the suffering you bring to this house. I pity you, Iphigenia, for your cruel fate. You do not deserve it.

(IPHIGENIA looks offstage.
The sound of men shouting
is heard and slowly gets
louder.)

IPHIGENIA
Mother, I see a man coming!

KLYTEMNESTRA
It is the son of a goddess, my girl, the man whom you came here to wed.

IPHIGENIA
I will have the servants help hide me.

KLYTEMNESTRA
Why do you want to hide, my child?

IPHIGENIA
I am ashamed of our ill-fated marriage.

KLYTEMNESTRA
There isn't time to be ashamed, right now. Stay, you can't afford to be overly modest. We must try our best.

(ACHILLES enters.)

ACIIILLES
Unhappy daughter of Leda—

KLYTEMNESTRA
You are right to call me unhappy.

ACHILLES
Do you hear the men's terrible cries?

KLYTEMNESTRA

What are they shouting about?

ACHILLES

About your daughter.

KLYTEMNESTRA

That is a bad omen.

ACHILLES

They say she must be sacrificed.

KLYTEMNESTRA

There's not a word of
disagreement?

ACHILLES

They shouted threats at me.

KLYTEMNESTRA

What sort of threats?

ACHILLES

To stone me to death.

KLYTEMNESTRA

For trying to save my daughter?

ACHILLES

Yes, for that.

KLYTEMNESTRA
Who would have dared to
attack you?

ACHILLES
Every one of them, together.

KLYTEMNESTRA
What about your own
Myrmidon soldiers?

ACHILLES
They would have joined the
attack. They would have
led it.

KLYTEMNESTRA
Oh, my girl, there is no hope.

ACHILLES
They mocked me for being a slave to marriage.

KLYTEMNESTRA
What did you respond?

ACHILLES
I told them not to kill my future wife.

KLYTEMNESTRA
Yes, that's your right.

ACHILLES

A wife who has been promised to me.

KLYTEMNESTRA

And brought to you from Argos.

ACHILLES

But I was drowned out by their shouts.

KLYTEMNESTRA

Mobs of men are horrible creatures.

ACHILLES

Nonetheless, I will stand by you.

KLYTEMNESTRA

Will you fight them on your own?

ACHILLES

A few loyal men will fight with me.

KLYTEMNESTRA

The gods will bless you for your efforts.

ACHILLES

Then I will be blessed.

KLYTEMNESTRA

So my daughter will not be sacrificed?

ACHILLES

Not if I can prevent it.

KLYTEMNESTRA

But will they come and try to take her?

ACHILLES

There will be thousands of them, led by Odysseus.

KLYTEMNESTRA

The son of Sisyphus?

*(ACHILLES peers offstage
to see if anyone's close.)*

ACHILLES

Yes, him.

KLYTEMNESTRA

Did he choose to do it, or was he chosen?

99

ACHILLES

Both.

KLYTEMNESTRA

An awful choice, to participate in murder.

ACHILLES

I will stop him.

KLYTEMNESTRA

Will he try to drag her away, against her will?

ACHILLES

By her hair, I am sure.

KLYTEMNESTRA

What should I do, if he does?

ACHILLES

Cling on to her.

KLYTEMNESTRA

I will. She will not be killed, if that happens.

ACHILLES

It will happen.

IPHIGENIA

Mother, listen to me. You are wrong to be angry with your husband, I see that now. There is no point in fighting the inevitable. We thank you, stranger, for your offer of help, but we cannot allow

you to face the wrath of the army. It will not help us, but it may harm you.

Listen to what I've been thinking, Mother. It seems clear to me that I must die. But I want to die gloriously, without a hint of dishonor. Consider what I'm saying, Mother. It is true. Our mighty country is looking to me, because those ships cannot sail to Troy and destroy it without my help. I can prevent those barbarians from ever again abducting our women. If they suffer for the abduction of Helen, whom Paris stole, they will not try to take our well-born wives again. My death will make sure of that. Achaea will be free, and my legendary name will be blessed for it.

I must not love my life too much. When I was born, I was born not just to you, but to our whole country. Innumerable soldiers and sailors are ready to fight courageously and die, because their country has been wronged. Should my one life stand in their way? Is that justice? Can we answer that?

Let me say one other thing. This man should not be forced to fight against our whole country for one woman's sake. One man's life is worth more than the lives of ten thousand women. If Artemis wants my body, who am I, a mortal, to oppose her? It's not possible. Here is my life—I give it to my country. Sacrifice me, and take down Troy. That will be my everlasting monument, my children, my marriage, my reputation. We must rule the barbarians. The barbarians cannot rule us. They are slaves. We must be free.

CHORUS LEADER

What you have said is noble, maiden. There is a sickness in the gods who have given you this fate.

ACHILLES

Daughter of Agamemnon, if I could have won you as my wife, it would have been a blessing from one of the gods. I envy our country for having you, and you for having our country. Your words are beautiful, worthy of Achaea. You have given up your battle against the gods, realizing their power, and instead chosen the most beneficial and necessary path. But now that I have seen your noble nature, I want to be your husband even more. Listen. I want to save you and take you home with me. Thetis my mother, witness the pain I feel because I cannot fight every Achaean there is to save Iphigenia. Think again: death is a terrible thing.

IPHIGENIA

Let me speak plainly, without fear of what anyone will say in response. It is enough that Helen is causing bloodshed with her beauty. As for you, stranger, do not die on my behalf, and do not kill. Let me save my country, if I can.

ACHILLES

What a noble heart you have. There is nothing more for me to say. You have made your decision. You have made a heroic choice—it is the truth, why not say it? Yet in case you change your mind, I will make you an offer: I will keep my weapons near the altar and be ready to save you from death. You may be brave, but when you are confronted with a knife at your throat, you will accept my help. I will not allow you to die because of a moment's recklessness. I will wait for you, armed, in the temple of the goddess.

(ACHILLES exits offstage.)

IPHIGENIA
Mother, why are you so silent and so sad?

KLYTEMNESTRA
The pain in my heart is all the reason I need.

IPHIGENIA
That is no reason. I am saved. I will honor your name.

KLYTEMNESTRA
What do you mean? Won't I mourn for you?

IPHIGENIA
No. I will have no grave.

KLYTEMNESTRA
If you are sacrificed, you will have a tomb.

IPHIGENIA
The altar of the goddess, the daughter of Zeus, will be my tomb.

KLYTEMNESTRA
That is true, my daughter. I will do as you wish.

IPHIGENIA
I am lucky to be able to serve my country.

KLYTEMNESTRA
What will I tell your sisters?

IPHIGENIA
Tell them not to mourn for me either.

KLYTEMNESTRA
Are there any final words of love you have for the girls?

IPHIGENIA
Tell them farewell. Tell them to raise Orestes to manhood.

KLYTEMNESTRA
In there anything in all Achaea I can do for you?

IPHIGENIA
Do not hate my father, your husband.

KLYTEMNESTRA
He will face a terrible future because of you.

IPHIGENIA
He did not want to bring me
to my end. He did it
for Achaea.

KLYTEMNESTRA
He used trickery, unworthy
of his father.

IPHIGENIA
Who will lead me to the
altar, so I am not dragged by
my hair?

KLYTEMNESTRA
I will take you—

IPHIGENIA
No, you won't. You shouldn't.

KLYTEMNESTRA
I will. I will cling to your robe.

IPHIGENIA
No, listen to me. It will be better for both of us if I let one of
my father's servants lead me to Artemis' meadow, where I will
be killed.

*(OLD SERVANT enters,
from the hut.)*

OLD SERVANT
Are you going from us, child?

IPHIGENIA
Yes. Never to return.

KLYTEMNESTRA
Will you leave your mother?

IPHIGENIA
As you see. Though you do not deserve it.

KLYTEMNESTRA
Don't go! Don't leave me!

IPHIGENIA
You must not weep.

CHORAL INTERLUDE 5

IPHIGENIA

Young women, let us sing to the glory of Artemis, daughter of Zeus!

Let the men of Achaea remain in reverent silence. Prepare the baskets, the barley, and the fire. Let my father begin his walk around the altar, going left to right.

For I will bring glory to my country and shelter it from harm.

Lead me forth, I am the destroyer of Troy!

Give me garlands for my head,
herc is my hair for your wreaths.
Bring forth the purifying water.

Let us dance to Artemis,
Artemis the queen, Artemis the blessed,

Let us dance round her temple and her altar.
Use my blood, the blood of my sacrifice,
to wash away any dark prophecy.

CHORUS

You call upon the city of Perseus,
the city built with Cyclopean labor.

IPHIGENIA

You raised me to be a light to my country.
I will not turn away from my death.

CHORUS

Your fame will last forever!

IPHIGENIA

Oh, bright light of day,
the very light of Zeus.
I go to a different light,
a different fate.
Goodbye, beloved light.

*(OLD SERVANT leads
IPHIGENIA offstage.)*

CHORUS

There she goes, the destroyer of Troy,
with garlands in her hair,
sprinkled by the purifying water,
ready to let blood gush onto the goddess's altar
out from her beautiful neck.
Your father's bountiful streams of pure water await you,
along with the army, eager for Troy.
Let us sing to Artemis, daughter of Zeus,
and ask her for good fortune.
Oh most reverend lady,
be pleased by this human sacrifice.
Send this army to treacherous Troy.
Let Agamemnon, with his spear,
put a wreath of deathless fame
upon the head of Achaea.

SCENE 6

*(OLD SERVANT enters
from offstage.)*

OLD SERVANT

Klytemnestra, daughter of Tyndareus, come out and hear
my message.

(KLYTEMNESTRA enters.)

KLYTEMNESTRA

I have heard you call, and here I am, full of sadness. I fear that
you have brought me new sorrows to add to my current ones.

OLD SERVANT

No, I have come to tell you a strange and
wonderful story about your daughter.

KLYTEMNESTRA

Go on, tell me at once.

OLD SERVANT

Beloved Queen, I will tell you everything,
as clearly as I can. I will start from the
beginning and continue on, unless my
memory falters and I stumble as I speak.

We went to the grove of Artemis, daughter of Zeus, where flowers adorn the ground. The army, which had been ordered to assemble, crowded in around us. King Agamemnon saw the girl approach the grove, groaned, and turned his head, hiding his tears with his robe. But the girl stood next to her father and said:

"Father, I have come to you of my own free will. I give my body to my country, to all Achaea. Bring me to the altar, if that's my fate. May you have luck, if I can give it. May you return home victorious. Do not take hold of me, my fellow Achaeans, I am brave enough to silently submit my throat."

This is what she said, and everyone marveled aloud at the girl's courage and nobility. From the midst of the crowd, Talthybius called for silence, as was his duty. Then Kalchas, the prophet, unsheathed a sharply honed knife, laying it in a golden basket. He set a wreath upon the girl's head. Achilles, son of Peleus, took the basket and a basin of purifying water and walked quickly round the altar, saying: "Artemis, daughter of Zeus, who brings death to wild beasts, who sends the bright orb of light through the night sky, accept this sacrifice which we Achaeans and Agamemnon offer you, this virgin blood from a pretty maiden's neck. Grant us smooth sailing and grant our spears the power to take down the towers of Troy."

As he spoke, the two sons of Artreus and all the army stood staring at the ground, and Kalchas took hold of the knife, looking close at the girl's throat and pondering where to cut. I stood with a bowed head and a heavy heart.

> *(The OLD SERVANT*
> *pauses, holding back tears.*
> *Then, suddenly, he smiles.)*

And then . . . a miracle! We clearly heard the blow strike, but the girl had vanished. Kalchas cried out, and the army echoed his cry of amazement at the unexpected sight, sent by the gods. It was something no one could have predicted or believed. There it was! A deer, huge and unmistakable, gasping its last breath, while its blood soaked the goddess's altar. As you can imagine, Kalchas shouted with joy, saying: "Achaean generals, do you see this sacrifice, this deer from the mountains, that the goddess has put upon her altar? She accepts this instead of the girl, instead of staining her altar with noble blood. She accepts it gladly and blesses our journey to attack Troy. Take heart, sailors, go to your ships, and get ready to leave the hollow bays of Aulis and cross the Aegean Sea!" Then, when Hephaistos's flames had consumed the sacrifice, Kalchas spoke the appropriate prayers for the army's safe return.

CHORUS LEADER

How wonderful to hear this message! He says the girl is still alive, among the gods!

KLYTEMNESTRA

Oh, my child. Which god has stolen you? How can I speak to you? Can I believe these foolish words I'm told to stop my bitter grief?

OLD SERVANT

King Agamemnon is coming. He will confirm the story.

(AGAMEMNON enters from offstage.)

AGAMEMNON

My wife, we should be happy for our daughter. She has the gods for company. But take our young calf here and go home. The soldiers are waiting to sail. Farewell. It will be a long time before I am able to greet you again, upon my return from Troy. I wish you well.

(AGAMEMNON exits.)

CHORUS

Rejoice, son of Atreus, you go to Troy. Rejoice. Some day you will return, bringing with you the spoils of war.

(KLYTEMNESTRA watches, silent.)

BLACKOUT

APPENDICES

ORIGINAL PRODUCTION
(APPENDIX A)

First performed at La MaMa's First Floor Theatre
74 E 4th St.
Feb 14 – Mar 3, 2013

Adapted and directed by Edward Einhorn
Music by Aldo Perez
Cheoreography by Patrice Miller
Art by Eric Shanower
Sets and masks by Jane Stein
Costumes by Carla Gant
Lighting by Jeff Nash

Presented by La MaMa in association with
Untitled Theater Company #61

With:

Amy Melissa Bentley (Attendant)
Lynn Berg (Servant)
Michael Bertolini (Agamemnon)
Ivanna Cullinan (Klytemnestra)
Giselle Chatelain (Attendant)
Laura Hartle (Iphigenia)
Paul Murillo (Achilles)
Eric Emil Oleson (Menelaus)
Jenny Lee Mitchell (Chorus Leader)
Sandy York (Chorus)
Emily Clare Zempel (Chorus)

Musicians:

Matthew Brundrett (drums)
Aldo Perez (guitar)
Mike Strauss (bass)

Stage Manager: Berit Johnson
Vocal Coach: Henry Akona
Assistant Director/Assistant Music Director: Daniela Hart
Fight Choreography: Dan Zisson
Asst Costume/Wardrobe: Jana Fronczek

More information about the production is available at
iphigeniainaulis.com

LA MAMA PRODUCTION: DIRECTOR'S NOTE
(APPENDIX B)

This appeared in the original program at La MaMa.

A few years ago, when reading my friend Eric Shanower's comic, *Age of Bronze* (his epic retelling of the Trojan War), I came across the story of Iphigenia's sacrifice. I vaguely remembered Euripides' play, but Eric's version highlighted themes that I found both compelling and surprisingly resonant. "It's all in Euripides," he told me. Reading the text again, there was much more in it than I remembered.

Eric and I started a graphic novel version of the play, using images from *Age of Bronze*—and we are still working on it. But once I had finished the translation, I wanted to stage it using images from Eric's work.

Iphigenia in Aulis is an examination of the power of the mob. The antagonists are not onstage: neither the soldiers that force the murder of Iphigenia, nor the prophet Kalchas who incites them, nor the rabble-rouser Odysseus who leads them. Instead we see Agamemnon and Klytemnestra struggle against fate—a fate determined not by the gods, but by an "angry horde of mortal men."

As a playwright, Euripides expresses an unusual level of doubt. Doubt about democracy, which is often a small step away from ochlocracy (mob rule) and doubt about religiously inspired violence. Such doubts resonate today, most recently in the revolutions of

the Arab Spring and their mixed consequences. Is democracy an unqualified good? When does it become a tyranny of the majority, or worse, a bloodthirsty force of a communal beast?

Although the antagonists are offstage, we see and hear a representative of the mob—the Chorus. The women of the Chorus straddle the border. They are part of "the masses," yet they also represent the oppressed—women raped or murdered in times of war. Their songs are violent, sexual, and raw, and rock is the obvious style to convey that energy. As a fan of Aldo Perez's music, I knew his style would allow the Chorus to be visceral, and even bestial, but also sexy and witty.

I deliberately mixed the language in this translation and gave the principals a heightened diction to set them apart from the Chorus. Their masks provide further distance, creating "second selves" that they serenely present in public, even while boiling with emotion inside. Jane Stein designed them to double as objects—a staff, a walking stick, a sword—that also conveyed status. For the faces, she transformed Eric's images into three dimensions that play on the historical links between masks, puppetry, and comic art.

Euripides' subject is surprisingly contemporary, and so is the way he tells it. The gods are mentioned, but their existence is ambiguous. Instead he focuses on men and the terrible acts they force each other to commit. This production intermingles the contemporary with the classical because Euripides' ideas are alive for us today, and just as deadly as they were 2,400 years ago.

THE LIVES OF 10,000 (APPENDIX C)

Every night in the theater, there was a moment which I know will get an audible reaction, sometimes a gasp, sometimes a snicker. After she has made the decision to let herself be sacrificed, Iphigenia proudly declares: "One man's life is worth more than the lives of ten thousand women."

Of course, it sounds ridiculous to us. It sounded ridiculous to me, as I translated the play, and I briefly considered if there was a way to make it more . . . palatable.

There wasn't.

But in rehearsals, I became fond of the line, in a perverse way.

In order for Iphigenia to make the transition from sacrifice to willing martyr, she has to truly believe and buy into everything she has been taught by her father and her society. That the Trojans are barbarians. That war means freedom. That a human sacrifice is a heroic martyrdom. And that a man's life is worth ten thousand women.

Somehow, we accept the other statements, because they are closer to statements we hear in our own society. But when we hear a statement that is clearly from another era, another mindset, it is jarring. It should be jarring. But it is of a piece. Just because some propaganda is longer lasting than others doesn't mean it isn't equally

propaganda. Snicker at it, perhaps, but then ask whether in a thousand years someone will be snickering at us.

Is *Iphigenia in Aulis* misogynist? Perhaps. It certainly is from a somewhat misogynist society, though there are aspects of the play, from Klytemnestra to the chorus, that have a more feminist outlook. The blaming and shaming of Helen has a sexist tinge, though it is of a piece with the societal shaming of adulterers; even Jason suffered for his betrayal of Medea.

And of course, sexism and misogyny exist in that society and our own in a thousand more subtle ways.

But that one line, to me, isn't misogynist. That line is a wake up call. Clearly, we see before us a woman whose life is worth at least as much as any man, perhaps more than many. Yet she has been formed by the society she is in, and she believes what the society believes.

In a play about the power of the mob, this is in fact the mob's greatest power. It lies not in its strength of arms, but in its conventional wisdom, in the banal but dangerous things everyone accepts, without questioning. Unless, perhaps, one had two and a half thousand years in which to reflect.

GLOSSARY OF NAMES

Pronunciation Guide

Stress italicized syllable

a as in lap

ay as in say

e as in bed

ee as in see

eye as in hike

g as in get

i as in sit

o as in not

oh as in note

oo as in wool

s as in less

th as in thick

u as in us

uh as in duh

Achaea a-*kee*-a, roughly the area now known as Greece; in the Bronze Age this area was divided into many smaller realms of varying sizes and strengths, each with its own king

Achilles a-*kil*-eez, son of Peleus and Thetis, prince of Phthia, the greatest of the Achaean warriors, also one of the youngest

Aenian *ee*-nee-an, from a region located near Lamia in modern Central Greece

Agamemnon a-ga-*mem*-non, king of Mycenae in the plain of Argos, High King of the Achaeans, leader of the Achaean army against Troy, husband of Klytemnestra, brother of Menelaus, son of Atreus

Ajax *ay*-jax, son of Telamon, prince of Salamis

Aphrodite a-froh-*deye*-tee, goddess of love

Apidanus a-pi-*day*-nus, a river in Phthia

Apollo a-*pol*-oh, god of the sun

Arethusa ar-e-*thyoo*-sa, a nymph, the daughter of Nereus

Argos *ar*-gos, wide Achaean plain dominated by the city of Mycenae

Artemis *ar*-te-mis, goddess of the hunt and moon

Asopos ay-*soh*-pos, a river god

Atreus *ay*-tryoos, father of Agamemnon and Menelaus

Athena a-*thee*-na, goddess of wisdom and war

Athens *a*-thenz, Achaean city in Attika, ruled by Menestheus

Aulis *aw*-lis, the bay and beach where the massive Achaean army assembles in preparation for sailing to attack Troy

Boeotia bee-*oh*-shuh, area north of Mycenae where Aulis is located

Centaurs *sen*-taurz, tribe of men that holds horses as holy, they are rumored to have the bodies of horses

Chalkis *kal*-kis, town on the shore of Euboea directly across the strait from Aulis

Cheiron *keye*-ron, centaur teacher of royal youths including young Achilles

Cyclops *seye*-klops, giant men born of Zeus, rumored to have built the massive walls of Mycenae

Echinae e-*keye*-nee, small coastal islands in the Ionean Sea

Eumelus yoo-*mee*-lus, an Achaean charioteer

Euripus *yoo*-ri-pus, strait on which Aulis is situated, dividing Boeotia from the Achaean mainland

Ganymedes ga-ni-*mee*-deez, great-uncle of King Priam of Troy; stolen as a youth by the thunder god, who admired his beauty, and taken to be wine-bearer to the gods

Guneus *goon*-yoos, king of Kyphus, one of the many Achaean kings who with his warriors joins the great Achaean army

Hades *hay*-deez, land of the dead, the underworld, also the name of the god of the underworld

Helen *he*-len, wife of Menelaus of Sparta before she ran away with Prince Paris of Troy, sister of Klytemnestra, daughter of Tyndareus and Leda

Hephaistos hee-*fays*-tos, lame smith god of fire

Hera *hee*-ra, queen of the gods

Hermione hur-*meye*-o-nee, daughter of Menelaus and Helen

Iphigenia i-fi-je-*neye*-a, first daughter of Agamemnon and Klytemnestra

Kadmus *kad*-mus, Achaean hero, former ruler of Thebes

Kalchas *kal*-kas, Trojan priest of the sun god, after the oracle at Delphi told him that Troy would fall he joins the Achaean army

Kassandra ka-*san*-druh, daughter of King Priam of Troy and his wife Hekuba, a seer

Kastor *kas*-tor, great Achaean hero, brother of Helen, twin of Pollux

Klytemnestra kleye-tem-*nes*-tra, wife of Agamemnon, sister of Helen, mother of Iphigenia

Kypris *kip*-ris, another name for Aphrodite, goddess of love

Leda *lee*-da, mother of Helen, Klytemnestra, Phoebe, Kastor, and Pollux; Leda was rumored to have been seduced by Zeus, king of the gods, and this union resulted in the birth of Helen and sometimes one or more of Leda's other children, depending on the version of the story

Libya *lib*-ee-a, a region west of the Nile, modern day Maghreb

Lydia *lid*-ee-a, a kingdom in western Asia Minor

Meges *me*-jeez, Achaean king of Dulichion

Menelaus me-ne-*lay*-us, king of Sparta in Lakedaemon, brother of Agamemnon, husband of Helen

Mycenae meye-*see*-nee, capital of Agamemnon in the plain of Argos, a city surrounded with walls so strong that people thought only the huge Cyclops could have raised the stones to build it. The famous monumental Lion Gate from the Bronze Age is still visible at Mycenae today.

Myrmidons *mur*-mi-donz, Achilles's soldiers from Phthia

Nereus *nee*-ree-us, Achaean god of ocean, reputed father of Thetis and grandfather of Achilles

Odysseus o-*dis*-yoos, Achaean king of Ithaka

Orestes oh-*res*-teez, son of Agamemnon and Klytemnestra

Paris *pa*-ris, Trojan prince, lover of Helen

Pelasgia pe-*laz*-gee-a, from the term deriving from Pelasgian, the indigenous inhabitants of Achaea and other lands surrounding the Aegean Sea

Peleus *peel*-yoos, Achaean king of Phthia, father of Achilles

Pelion *pee*-lee-on, mountain abode of Cheiron

Pelops *pel*-ops, paternal grandfather of Agamemnon and Menelaus

Perseus *per*-syoos, great Achaean hero, first ruler of Mycenae

Pharsalus far-*say*-lus, capital city of the kingdom of Myrmidons, ruled by Peleus, father of Achilles

Phoebe *fee*-bee, sister of Helen and Klytemnestra

Phrygia *fri*-ja, area northeast of Troy

Phthia *ftheye*-a, Achaean area in Thessaly ruled by Peleus, home of Achilles and the Myrmidons

Pleiades *plee*-a-deez, group of seven stars, known as the seven sisters

Pollux *po*-luks, great Achaean hero, brother of Helen, twin of Kastor

Priam *preye*-am, king of Troy

Salamis *sa*-la-mis, Achaean island ruled by Telamon

Sirius *si*-ree-us, the brightest star in the sky, the eye in the constellation of the dog

Simois *si*-moh-is, a river in the plain before Troy

Sisyphus *sis*-i-fus, Corinthian hero who outwitted the gods and was sentenced after death to forever push a stone up a hill in the underworld only to have it roll to the bottom when he neared the summit, sometimes called the father of Odysseus because Odysseus often displays a similar tricky intellect

Sparta *spar*-tuh, Achaean city in Lakedaemon ruled by Menelaus

Talthybius tal-*thi*-bee-us, herald of Agamemnon

Tantalus *tan*-ta-lus, great-grandfather of Agamemnon and Menelaus

Taphian *taf*-yan, from the island of Taphos, in the Ionian Sea, and considered to be pirates by nature

Thessaly *thes*-a-lee, Achaean area inhabited by the Aeolians

Thestius *thes*-tee-us, maternal grandfather of Helen and Klytemnestra

Thetis *thee*-tis, influential Achaean priestess, mother of Achilles, former wife of Peleus, daughter of Nereus the Ocean

Troy troy, city of the Trojans on the northwest point of Asia Minor

Tyndareus tin-*dar*-yoos, father of Helen, Klytemnestra, Phoebe, Kastor, and Pollux

Zeus zyoos, god of thunder and sky

GENEALOGICAL CHART: THE ACHAEANS

Characters in bold appear in *Iphigenia in Aulis*.

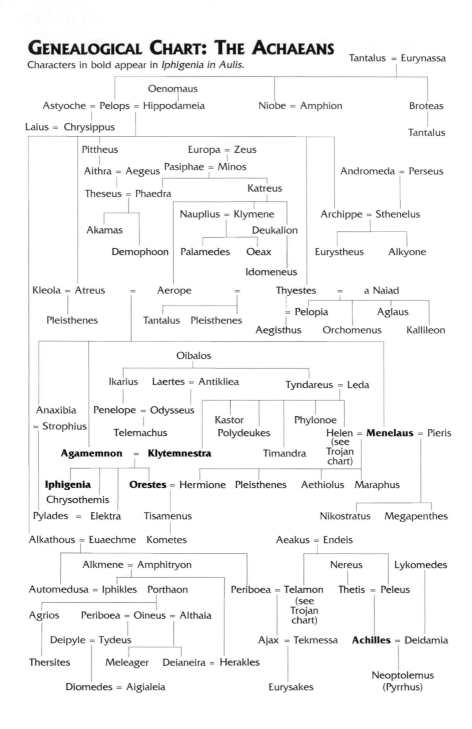

GENEALOGICAL CHART: THE TROJAN ROYAL FAMILY

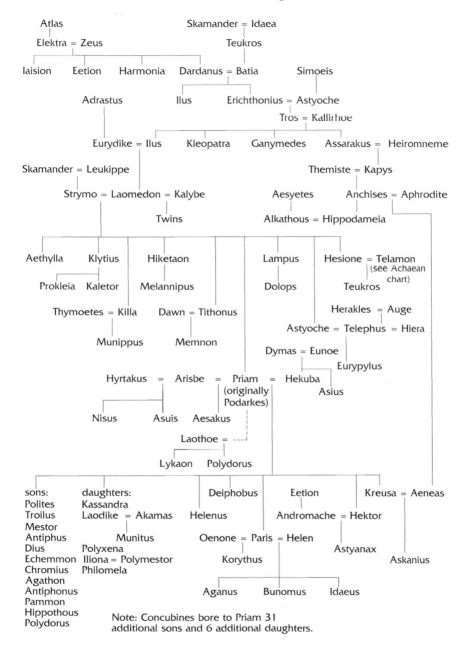

Atlas

Skamander = Idaea

Elektra = Zeus

Teukros

Iaision   Eetion   Harmonia   Dardanus = Batia   Simoeis

Adrastus   Ilus   Erichthonius = Astyoche

Tros = Kallirhoe

Eurydike = Ilus   Kleopatra   Ganymedes   Assarakus = Heiromneme

Skamander = Leukippe   Themiste = Kapys

Strymo = Laomedon = Kalybe   Aesyetes   Anchises = Aphrodite

Twins   Alkathous = Hippodameia

Aethylla   Klytius   Hiketaon   Lampus   Hesione = Telamon
                                                    (see Achaean
                                                    chart)

Prokleia   Kaletor   Melannipus   Dolops   Teukros

Thymoetes = Killa   Dawn = Tithonus   Herakles = Auge

Munippus   Memnon   Astyoche = Telephus = Hiera

Dymas = Eunoe

Eurypylus

Hyrtakus = Arisbe = Priam = Hekuba   Asius
                    (originally
                    Podarkes)

Nisus   Asuis   Aesakus

Laothoe = ---

Lykaon   Polydorus

sons: daughters: Deiphobus   Eetion   Kreusa = Aeneas
Polites   Kassandra
Troilus   Laodike = Akamas   Helenus   Andromache = Hektor
Mestor
Antiphus   Munitus   Oenone = Paris = Helen
Dius   Polyxena
Echemmon   Iliona = Polymestor   Korythus   Astyanax   Askanius
Chromius   Philomela
Agathon
Antiphonus
Pammon   Aganus   Bunomus   Idaeus
Hippothous   Note: Concubines bore to Priam 31
Polydorus   additional sons and 6 additional daughters.

Eric Shanower is the award-winning cartoonist of the graphic novel series *Age of Bronze* (Image Comics), retelling the story of the Trojan War. He wrote *New York Times* best-selling graphic novel adaptations of L. Frank Baum's Oz books (Marvel Comics) and the Eisner Award-winning comics series *Little Nemo: Return to Slumberland* (IDW). Shanower's past comics work includes his own Oz graphic novel series, available as *Adventures in Oz* (IDW), the story "Happily Ever After" included in the Lambda Literary Award finalist *How Beautiful the Ordinary* (HarperCollins), and art for *An Accidental Death* by Ed Brubaker (Fantagaphics Books), *The Elsewhere Prince* by Moebius and R-JM Lofficier (Marvel), and Harlan Ellison's *Dream Corridor* (Dark Horse Comics). Shanower has illustrated for television, magazines, and children's books, two of which he wrote himself. He lives in Portland, Oregon.

Edward Einhorn is a playwright, director, translator, librettist, and novelist. He writes plays about neurology; stage adaptations of science fiction novels; translations of plays written in French, Czech, and ancient Greek; puppet theater; modern Oz novels (illustrated by Eric Shanower); picture books about math; opera/oratorio librettos; and other texts of a less definable nature. *The New York Times* has called his work "exquisitely ingenious," "dramatically shrewd," and "almost unbearably funny"; *Time Out* has called it "challenging, thought-provoking," "mesmerizing," and "startlingly intense"; and *The Village Voice* has called it "hilarious, provocative," and "inspired absurdist comedy." He has received a Sloan Grant, *SEED Magazine*'s Revolutionary Mind Award, and Critic's Picks in *Time Out*, *The Village Voice*, and *The New York Times*. This is his second Greek translation/adaptation, the first being *Lysistrata*. He is the Artistic Director of Untitled Theater Company No. 61, in New York.